Jarvais Po
The secret adventures of a potato

The Garden Bunch Series

By Abesi Manyando
Illustrations by Fuuji Takashi

© Abesi Manyando, 2020

All rights reserved. No part of this book may be reproduced or utilized in any form or by any means, electronic or mechanical, including photocopying, recording, or by any information storage and retrieval system, without permission in writing from the author.

First published in 2020

Written by Abesi Manyando
Illustrations by Fuuji Takashi
Book layout by Bryony van der Merwe

ISBN: 978-1-7363740-0-9 (paperback edition)

Published by 7th and Lotus
website: www.thegardenbunch.com

Dedication

For the children too afraid to go to school,
too afraid to sit in the cafeteria,
maybe too afraid to go home,
may you find your power.

This book is dedicated to my grandmother, Abesi, my grandfather,
Moses R. Sambo, and my God Mother, Eva Tagger.
May we meet again in another life, in another garden.
Thank you for your love.

INTRO
Harvest Farm

It was a very hot Sunday morning at Harvest Farm. Mrs Harvest was still sound asleep but her husband and her daughter, Hope, were not.

Mr Harvest was outside tending to his crops. Hope Harvest was in her bedroom, staring out of the window and into the garden. She was thinking about her grandmother who had recently left the farm because she became ill. When she said goodbye, her grandmother had asked Hope for a special favor.

"Fruit, vegetables, flowers and plants are very important to the earth and to me," her grandmother told her. "They are magical. They are Our Garden Bunch. You must look after them for me and protect them."

Hope had done exactly this. And whenever she missed her grandmother, Hope went to the garden and found her happiness there. It was very magical indeed.

Chapter 1: Everyday Struggle

Mr Harvest had been waiting for it to rain. But for weeks no rain had come, so he decided to water his crops that early morning. Little did he know that his crops had started their day hours before. Hope was carefully watching them through her window.

Jarvais 'Po' Potato was supposed to be listening to Mrs Georgia Louise Peach sing her life away during the Sunday choir selection at Garden Green for All Fellowship. Instead, he was daydreaming about what his life would have been like if he hadn't been born a Potato.

Life had never been easy for Jarvais. As far as he could remember, his entir-r-r-e-e life had been a struggle! Out of all the Fruits and Vegetables at Harvest Farm, the Potatoes were the smallest group and the least important; at least that's what Jarvais thought.

And the past few days had been particularly rough for Jarvais.

Jarvais' mind flashed back to Saturday, when Mr Harvest moved in a new family of Potatoes. Jarvais' family had been helping them move when Katarina Carrot's parents walked by with the Strawberry family.

"Oh, my!" exclaimed Mrs Carrot loudly. "It looks like more and more Potatoes are moving in."

"There goes the neigh-bor-hood," complained Mr Carrot. "Pretty soon we won't be a respectable looking farm."

"My, my, with all the gorgeous Strawberries in the world, I can't imagine why Mr Harvest wastes his time with these funny-looking Potatoes," snickered Mrs Strawberry. "They are so dull and drabby. He could have at least picked the ones that are red, like us."

"Oh, please," said Mrs Carrot, turning up her nose. "Red, yellow, brown, blue, pale or purple. A Potato is a Potato. They just don't fit in with the look of our farm."

Mrs Strawberry and the Carrots didn't even bother whispering. Mr Strawberry seemed embarrassed by his wife's behavior and kept his head down.

The Potatoes heard what was said, but they just went about their business and ignored the insults and chatter.

But Jarvais couldn't ignore it. He was furious.

"Dad, you should've said something!" he exclaimed.

"There is nothing to say," said his father calmly. "We know who we are. We don't need them to verify our worth."

"Veri… what dad? I don't get it. It seems like every Potato here believes that they really are worthless. We never stand up for ourselves and we're always quiet and forgiving. That's so weak," shouted Jarvais.

"Jarvais, maybe you're the one who believes you're worthless," explained his father. "You're the only one who reacts to this nonsense. All the other Potatoes probably **know** their value. Someone once said, *No one can make you feel inferior without your consent.*"

"Does *inferior* mean *bad*?" asked Jarvais.

"No, it means *less than*," said his father. "You have great value, just like your mother always tells you. You're very powerful and if you don't believe anything else, believe that. It's a big world out there. Don't ever forget that. No matter where you go."

"Okay, okay, okay," said Jarvais. "I get it."

Jarvais decided to go find his best friend, Brea Broccoli. He cleaned himself up, changed clothes and walked over to Brea's stunning Broccoli house. He wasn't about to waste a good Saturday feeling down.

"I wish I could just leave this farm altogether," he told Brea.

"What?" Brea yelled. Brea's mom and dad were reggae musicians. And today the band was practicing in the house.

"For the third time, I said I wish I could leave this farm."

"Why would you want to do that?" yelled Mrs Broccoli from the living room, dancing along to the music.

Jarvais told Brea's parents what happened with Mrs Strawberry and the Carrots.

"Being a Potato is an endless struggle," moaned Jarvais. "I wish Potatoes could be great like Strawberries, Broccolis, Carrots, Celery, Apples, Mangoes and all the other Fruits and Vegetables, just like Mrs Carrot said."

"Ah, young Jarvais, don't worry yourself about the opinions of other produce. One must explore the intent of a person's words, man," said Brea's dad, smiling. "There is a proverb that says, *Until the lion has its own storyteller, the hunter will always be the hero of the story*."

Jarvais was more confused than ever. *Lions? Lions? Who said anything about lions?* he thought. *Geez!* Brea's house was no place to talk about the future, he concluded.

Jarvais and Brea went outside. They hid between the blades of grass and watched Mr Harvest load his truck. They often did this on Saturday mornings, and wondered where Mr Harvest went.

Jarvais had always wanted to find out but his parents told him to never leave the farm without them.

Jarvais was feeling inquisitive, though. The day already started off bad and he wanted to experience the big world that his father had mentioned. Harvest Farm was in a small town in South Garden. It was forty-five minutes away from New Garden. That's where Market City and all the action was.

"I gotta get out of here. This can't be life, Brea. We should sneak into one of those boxes," suggested Jarvais.

"But how are we going to make sure we get back alright?" asked Brea.

"Oh, I didn't think about that," answered Jarvais.

Then they heard Aaliyah Fuji Apple singing. They could hear her voice was coming towards them, but they couldn't see her.

"It's too bad you guys aren't me," said Aaliyah Apple.

Brea and Jarvais could see Hope Harvest's shoes in the grass but they still couldn't see Aaliyah. When Hope put her bag on the ground, Aaliyah popped out and bowed gracefully like a ballerina.

"Oh, there you are," said Brea.

"Hey guys, if you want to see where we're going, you can come with me," said Aaliyah. You'll be safe. Hope takes me everywhere. I'm her favorite fruit. Straw Eri is here, too."

Jarvais felt tense when Aaliyah mentioned her name. *Oh gosh, not Straw Eri Strawberry of all Fruits*, Jarvais thought. *She was no better than her mother.*

Still, Jarvais wasted no time hopping inside Hope's bag with Brea. It was nice and comfy. They settled in next to some books, making sure they could see everything.

Straw was lying back, sipping water. She looked at Brea and Jarvais when they came inside and then looked away without saying anything.

"Have some water, too. It will balance you out and keep you healthy," recommended Aaliyah.

"Th-tha-thank you, Aa-Ah-Aaliyah," responded Jarvais, stuttering. He was always a little nervous around Aaliyah and never hung out with her outside of school.

"It's what I do. My dad is a doctor so I'm a health expert, amongst other things," said Aaliyah. Before she could continue, Straw interrupted.

"So Jarvais, you know Aaliyah and I are all about *that* life – first class trips, overseas vacations, parties on foreign farms. Cars, planes, yachts, you name it. We've been around the world and back three times," bragged Straw Eri. "We were just in Broccoli City last week with my Dad. The city was lit up, it was like a movie. We were jumping on go-carts that turn into jets. We flew all **over** the city."

"Oh really," questioned Brea, her eyebrows raised. "I'll be sure to ask my cousins if they saw you."

"It was super crowded, Brea," Straw Eri snapped. "I doubt they did. But yeah, the perks of being a Strawberry and an Apple are endless. It's the life, I tell you!"

Aaliyah winked at Jarvais and smiled. Brea looked at Jarvais, too. He seemed absolutely mesmerized by their stories. He barely blinked. Brea crossed her arms and ran her hands through her pretty Broccoli crown of curls. "What did I get myself into?" she whispered, sighing heavily and rolling her eyes.

Jarvais was listening to Straw Eri and Aaliyah's every word. He could only imagine what a different life Strawberries and Apples lived in comparison to Potatoes. Aaliyah talked the whole time like a tour guide, but Jarvais didn't mind. He had never been in a car before and he liked Aaliyah. She was really smart. Everyone liked her even though she was the teacher's pet. Aaliyah was Brea's friend, and although he didn't speak much to her at school, she wasn't mean to him like Cee Celery and his clique.

Cee Celery was brutal and he loved picking on Jarvais and others. He was always trying to impress Ella Eggplant, Katarina Carrot and his followers. He really bullied Jarvais more than anyone. This was another reason that Jarvais wished he wasn't a Potato.

Jarvais could tell that they arrived somewhere exciting. The car stopped and suddenly they were outside. He saw shoes walking everywhere. It was noisy and crowded. Brea put her hands over her ears.

"Brea, we're in Market City. Look at all the different Fruits and Vegetables here," said Aaliyah.

Jarvais and Brea both stared through Hope's bag.

"Wow," exclaimed Jarvais. "This is incredible!"

As Hope followed her father through the market, Aaliyah and Straw Eri gave Brea and Jarvais a tour of Market City.

"Wow, Fruits and Vegetables here live really close together; like on top of each other," said Jarvais.

"Yeah, the buildings are called skyscrapers, Jarvais. My cousins live in a penthouse over their on 5th Avenue," Aaliyah said, pointing to a street that was filled with luxurious skyscrapers.

Jarvais' eyes grew as big as frisbees. He saw that most of the red fruits like Strawberries, Apples and other Berries lived in the beautiful square-shaped penthouses. Pineapples lived in spacious houses on the Upper Pine Side. Guavas, Mangoes, Coconuts and Bananas lived in amazing Condos on Tropical Street and 7th Avenue near the Oranges.

"I think my aunt and uncle own that Vegan Theater on 4th Avenue and Grace Street," said Brea.

"My dad knows the Rutabaga who bought up a lot of these properties," said Straw Eri.

"Well, he didn't buy my family's property," snapped Brea. Straw Eri always had to come out on top no matter what, and Brea was getting annoyed.

"Anyway, Brea, the Broccolis, Cauliflowers and Brussels Sprouts all live around 4th Avenue across from the Mushrooms."

The avenue was a busy art district with multi-colored apartment buildings. Some of the Broccolis waved at Brea. She could see paintings of her dad for sale on several corner stands. Brea went from being annoyed to excited. She never allowed anyone to ruin her day or change her character, not even Straw Eri.

"Wow, we're definitely not on Harvest Farm anymore!" exclaimed Jarvais.

4th Avenue was next to Green Street and 5th, where the Lettuce, Kale and Spinach lived in massive lofts designed like ice cubes. Cucumbers lived nearby. Green Street was surrounded by gorgeous fountains. Everything seemed to be so much larger than life.

"It's like a movie," said Jarvais. "It makes our farm feel so small."

"Look over there, guys. They are probably Que Cumbers cousins," Aaliyah laughed as she pointed at a loud group of sour pickles arguing across the street. "Don't they look so silly, just like Que?"

Jarvais looked and smiled a little. He thought he and Brea were the only ones who couldn't stand Que Cumber. He and Tommy Tomato were Cee Celery's sidekicks. He often teased Jarvais by saying that he was ugly, yet he was funny-looking himself.

All of the apartments, condos and homes were beautifully designed in Market City. Everyone's place seemed to be made of glass or a pretty transparent material that you could see through.

"This is it!" said Aaliyah.

"I love it!" exclaimed Jarvais. "I hope one day I get to live here too."

"Wait a minute," said Brea loudly. "Wait one good minute. We didn't see any Potatoes. I'm sure Jarvais has relatives here somewhere."

"Aww, Jarvais, yeah. I almost forgot," said Straw Eri with a strange grin on her face. "The Potatoes live on the other side of the street. Look."

"I don't see any penthouses or apartments," said Jarvais, confused.

"Look lower," urged Straw Eri. "Over by the abandoned buildings."

"But that just looks like a bunch of old sacks," said Jarvais. "No one can live there."

"That's exactly where Potatoes live. Red Potatoes, Sweet Potatoes, Purple Potatoes, all Potatoes. Right over there," said Straw Eri. "Look at the sack building, it even says so."

Jarvais' smile disappeared and his heart dropped. Straw Eri was right. He wished it wasn't true but he could see it with his own eyes. Jarvais felt like someone had cut him with a knife.

No, this can't be where the Potatoes live, he thought. *Why would only the Potatoes live in such a condition, where you couldn't even see their apartments and homes? Where they seemed to be overcrowded without an inch of space to move around and run freely like on Harvest Farm.*

Jarvais looked down feeling sad and ashamed.

"But I always heard about the Potato District," he said as he coughed and held back tears. "That's where Potato Glow is. It's, um, a really pretty district where a lot of Potatoes live. I thought it was somewhere here in Market City."

"Sorry, but that's not real," said Straw Eri. "That's just a story someone made up."

"Are you sure?" asked Aaliyah. "There are lots of districts in Market City. The city has different parts."

"Yeah, but we've been to every part with Hope. It's not a real place," said Straw Eri. "I even asked my mom and she said it wasn't real. When I asked Mrs Carrot, she said, 'Have you ever learned about this make-believe place in history or geography class?' Well, have we?"

Straw Eri waited for the three of them to answer. But they couldn't, because for once, she was right.

After a minute passed Aaliyah spoke. "But the buildings behind the Potato sack building look like …"

Straw Eri cut Aaliyah off quickly. "I'm over this!" she yelled, fuming with anger. Her face was red. "This is where all the Potatoes come from and where they live, period!"

Aaliyah and Brea looked away. The seconds felt like hours to Jarvais as the four of them stood in silence, completely shocked.

Then they heard Mr Harvest's voice, "C'mon Hope, why are you standing by this old aisle in a daze. They're renovating over here. Let's go, I'm done."

Chapter 2
It's gonna take a miracle!

"Look at how he works when you give him all your praise, Greater Garden!" shouted Pastor George Peach Senior in his deep country southern drawl. "Sing, Garden sing," he urged the choir. Jarvais had been so busy thinking about what happened yesterday that he almost forgot where he was.

Mrs Georgia Louise Peach was singing at the top of her lungs like she did in class. "Melodies from heaven, rain down on me," she sang through sweat and tears, dabbing her forehead with a handkerchief.

Brea's dad, who was the special guest, was playing his guitar and adding his own Reggae melodies to the song. He was joined by the Soweto Mass Produce Choir and the legendary Cauliflower Sisters. Everyone was jamming along, except Jarvais.

"Somebody is in need of a miracle and prayer today," shouted Pastor George Peach Senior.

"Yes, yes," chanted the elder Fruits.

"I know you're there," repeated Pastor Peach. "Greater Garden, I said somebody is in need of a miracle. You've been waiting for that change. Your breakthrough is here. Won't you come?"

The music got faster and faster as the energy elevated inside the building. Some Fruits were shouting, and some Vegetables were clapping and shaking. Usher Orange D O.'dell Day, who was near Jarvais, started dancing like her feet were on fire.

"Somebody is in need of a miracle today, Garden. I know you're there," hollered Pastor Peach. "Come on, somebody!"

Usher Orange D. O'dell Day was jumping up and down and lost control. She swung one hand over Jarvais shoulder and when she touched him, he shot right up.

"Yessss, Jarvais, yessss."

Usher Orange D. O'dell Day screamed with excitement and flung her arms wide open, hugging Jarvais. Before he could respond she dragged him to the front.

"Yessssss, yessssss, yes!" she yelled through tears of excitement.

"Come on up here, young Jarvais. Leave your trooouuuubles at the altar. What is on your mind?" asked Pastor Peach.

Jarvais looked up at Pastor Peach and looked down thinking about all his problems.

"Well," Jarvais finally answered, "my trouble is simple."

"Alright now, there's nothing he can't handle," said Mrs Georgia Louise Peach, smiling proudly at Jarvais.

"Okay, I hate being a Potato. I wish I could be something else. That's it," said Jarvais.

The music stopped as the band froze in silence. Pastor Peach was speechless. His eyes were big like two basketballs. Mother Banana and Usher Orange D. O'dell Day looked at each other in shock. The legendary Cauliflower Sisters all fainted in the same direction… at the same time. All the Fruits and Vegetables fell silent. Finally, Jarvais' mother stood up and threw her hands up in the air as if she were defeated. "Somebody help this child of mine." She almost fainted but was startled by Mrs Georgia Louise Peach's scream.

"Oh my gawd!" screamed Mrs Georgia Louise Peach, looking up at the sky. "It is truly raining down on us. Well, Greater Garden, let us quickly pass the collection basket, and I mean expeditiously pass the collection, and exit as it is time to go, Saints."

And it was. Everyone rushed out of service. Jarvais was saved by the rain and his teacher.

What the crops thought was rain was actually Mr Harvest watering the garden. It had been a long time since they'd had real rain. Later that evening, Mr Harvest left the sprinklers on as Hope watched the crops from her window.

It was a quiet night in Jarvais' home. His parents were very hurt by his behavior at service, and they spent the evening watching what they thought was rain from their window. Jarvais was in his bed. He knew his parents were deeply disappointed. "But what do they know?" Jarvais said to himself. They had no idea what he experienced the day before at Market City or the horror he faced at school every single day, when Cee Celery bullied him.

Jarvais had been picked on so much by Cee Celery that when Brea or his good friend, Alvin Avocado, didn't come to school, he would eat lunch in the bathroom corner because he was so afraid.

Last Friday, Jarvais was at his locker and he saw Brea, Alvin Avocado and Aaliyah Apple on the other side. He was about to walk over to them when Cee Celery cornered him. He was with Que Cumber, Tommy Tomato and Ella Eggplant. Jarvais' heart started beating very fast. He tried to walk away quickly, holding his books and head low, and hoping that maybe today, just today, Cee celery would leave him alone. That wasn't happening. The hallway was crowded. It was just what Cee Celery enjoyed … an audience!

"Hey, Jarrrrrvaaaiisss," yelled Cee Celery.

Jarvais refused to look up.

Cee Celery called him again, "Hey, you little spotty-skinned tuber!"

Before he knew it, Cee Celery had slammed him into the lockers. "How do you like your Potatoes, Jarvais? Smaaaasssshed?" teased Celery.

Que Cumber and Tommy Tomato erupted in laughter as they proudly walked away. Ella Eggplant looked the other way, like the rest of Jarvais's schoolmates in the hall.

Jarvais' head was spinning in pain and his books were all over the floor. Brea ran to him and started picking up his books. Alvin Avocado wheeled himself behind her. Aaliyah Apple yelled for Mrs Georgia Louise Peach. By the time Mrs Peach came, Cee Celery was gone and no one said anything.

"Jarvais, are you okay?" asked Mrs Peach.

Jarvais' head was still spinning and his body was in terrible pain.

"I'm okay," Jarvais responded. It didn't matter anymore. It was just another day in the uneasy life of Jarvais Po.

On Monday, Jarvais pleaded with his Mom to let him stay home. He used to love school but now he dreaded going. Every morning, he had a million excuses to not go. He would say he had a Potato ache or hay fever but his mother never bought it. She would always advise, "You have to get an education so you can make something out of your life." *It's not like I'm ever going to amount to being anything but a boring dull Potato with spotty skin,* he thought.

That Monday, Mrs Georgia Louise Peach announced that the class would be taking a field trip to Market City, New Garden. This made Jarvais more nervous than before. If the trip was going to be like what he experienced over the weekend, he knew Cee Celery was really going to have a ball bullying him. Jarvais was terrified.

Market City was packed. There were buildings everywhere, way bigger than what Jarvais had seen on his previous visit. Jarvais, Brea, Aaliyah, Straw Eri and Alvin were at the end of the line making sure they kept their distance from Cee Celery and Que Cucumber. The class explored the city, going from place to place. At lunch time, Mrs Louise Peach took them to McVeggies near Manya's Square Garden. It was really crowded inside.

Jarvais, Brea, Alvin and Aaliyah were the last to order their food. They stood in line as Bianca Beet asked them what they wanted. As Jarvais was thinking, Alvin Avocado pointed at a sign on top of the menu. "Look, Jarvais, Made in Potato Glow. I guess it is a real place after all."

"No, Straw Eri said it wasn't real," Jarvais replied. He quietly ordered a hot bowl of seed soup and started walking to the lunch table with his friends.

MADE IN POTATO GLOW

Before Jarvais reached the table, Cee Celery walked towards him, with Que Cumber and Tommy Tomato following. When Alvin Avocado tried to block him, he pushed Alvin's wheelchair to the side causing Brea and Aaliyah to fall. He smiled wildly and then tripped Jarvais. Jarvais fell and his bowl of soup went up in the air and landed on his head. Cee Celery laughed and pretended to help Jarvais up.

"And they all fall like dominoes," Cee Celery sang as he laughed. Then he asked Que and Tommy, "What do you call a Potato burning up?"

"We don't know," they responded slowly.

"A hot Potato or, better yet, a b-a-a-a-a-k-k-ed Potato. So many options, I don't know what to do with myself," chuckled Cee Celery.

He had a good isolated laugh and then walked away. Jarvais wiped the soup from his eyes and saw that everyone was looking at him. Some were even recording him on their cell phones. They walked past as Brea handed him some napkins.

Jarvais' skin felt like it was burning. He was so humiliated. He got up and ran out of McVeggies. He didn't know where he was going. He just ran. Brea, Alvin and Aaliyah yelled for him to come back. But it was too late.

Jarvais ran and ran until he was out of breath. He stopped at a bus station by Market Square to rest. When he looked up he saw a sign that said, *A line to Potato Avenue*. Jarvais' eyes grew big. He saw his friends coming up the road, so he hid. He wasn't ready to go back to his classmates.

There were three distinguished Potatoes waiting for the bus, and talking to a Rutabaga.

"The bus is running late today. Traffic must be really bad in Potato Glow," said one of the Potatoes. "Everybody from around the world has been coming to the annual festival for years. You would think they would've figured out the traffic issue by now."

"I'm gonna fix this city's transport problem with my new tech transport. I'm gonna connect all the boroughs from here to Broccoli City and to the farms. Every city will glow like Potato Glow when I'm done," said the awkward-looking round Rutabaga.

"Potato Glow?" asked Jarvais. "Is it a real place after all?"

"Of course! It's the reason everyone comes to Market City," said another Potato.

"Market City is home of the Potato District, known as Potato Glow. It's the greatest district on earth if you ask me. Lots of history, lots of art, lots of music."

"Wow, but Straw Eri and her mom said it wasn't real and when we came to Market City, the Potatoes lived … um, in a … well, not such a nice part."

"You mean where all the renovations are going on, kid? Heck, that's one small section and there are other buildings right behind the older Potato buildings. As a matter fact, the old Strawberry High Rise that's being torn down is right behind. I bet your friend didn't show you that. Mr Rudy Rutabaga is rebuilding that whole area. I don't know who you've been listening to, son, but Potato Glow is real and it is beautiful. Everyone comes here this time of year to see the annual Potato Glow Arts and History Festival," he said.

"All all these Fruits and Vegetables are here for the Potato Festival?" Jarvais asked.

"Of course," the Potato responded.

Wow. Jarvais wondered why Straw Eri had lied to him. Maybe she didn't know the truth. He thought about all the things everyone said about Potatoes and how those things had made him feel not good enough.

Jarvais sat there in awe. What if everything he thought about himself had all been a lie? Had he defined himself by what was never real to begin with?

"All this time, I thought that I didn't want to be a Potato because of a lie," he said out loud.

"If you think your life is hard, little runt, try being a Rutabaga for a day. You have no idea what that's like."

The grumpy round Rutabaga threw a newspaper at Jarvais and walked away. The paper headline read *Potato Glow Festival breaks attendance records!*

Before Jarvais could say thank you, the agitated Rutabaga got into a plush SUV with some Turnips wearing construction hats.

"I want all the lights to turn purple at 1:30," ordered the Rutabaga to a group of Cabbages and Turnips who looked like engineers. He was yelling out of his window very loudly. "The city's gonna glow. It's gonna be the biggest light show on earth! Huge numbers!" he exclaimed as he was chauffeured away. "Huge huge numbers!"

The Potatoes looked at the Rutabaga and shook their heads. As the bus came nearer, Jarvais saw Brea, Alvin, Aaliyah and Straw Eri headed his way.

"Jarvais, we've been looking everywhere for you. Where are you going?" asked Brea.

"I'm getting on this bus to 7th and Lotus, and I'm going to The Potato Museum of History and Arts in Potato Glow for the festival. Nothing's going to stop me," said Jarvais.

"Oh, no, no, no, we're *all* going to Potato Glow. That's why we came to Market City."

Jarvais looked up and saw Mrs Georgia Louise Peach. She wiped the sweat off her forehead as she nervously tried to catch her breath.

"We're all gonna learn some real good, good history today," she said. "But first, let's all go back to McVeggies. We're gonna eat our heavenly nutritious meals and be on our way to the Potato Museum."

She made it a point to keep her eyes on Jarvais for the rest of the trip.

The ride to the Potato District was astonishing. Jarvais couldn't believe how colorful and rich it was. The buildings and homes were so artistic and creative. There were Potatoes everywhere, along with other Fruits and Veggies.

CHAPTER 3
The Miseducation

Potato Glow was filled with music, art and a lot of technology and lights, just like the Rutabaga had said. Jarvais noticed hundreds of lights on top of the museum.

The museum was massive with high ceilings and the most amazing art and science displays that Jarvais had ever seen. The two Potatoes that Jarvais had met at the bus stop were leading the museum tour that the class was on. Their names were Mr Granda and Mr Uri.

Jarvais learned that Potatoes had a rich history dating all the way back to 2500 B.C. "According to historians, the introduction of the Potato was responsible for a quarter of the growth in the old world population and urbanization between 1700 and 1900. Potatoes were the principal energy source for the Inca civilization. Following the Spanish conquest of the Inca, the Potato was introduced to Europe in the second half of the 16th century," explained Mr Uri.

They also learned that people love Potatoes because they are dependable, rich in starch and always available.

"There was a famine one time in Ireland called the Potato Famine," Mr Granda told them. "This was a very difficult time for the Potato population." He started choking up a little and Mr Uri had to finish the story.

As Mr Uri was talking, Mrs Georgia Louise Peach kept looking out of the window. It was getting cloudy and a bit dark outside.

Mr Harvest and Hope were going from place to place at the Potato Farmers Market in the city. Suddenly the sky went from being sunny to dark. Rain was finally on its way.

"It's been a long time coming," Mr Harvest said to Hope. But Hope wasn't listening. She was in her own world across the aisle singing along to the afrobeat playlist on her little speaker. When her battery light came on, she panicked. "Oh no, I gotta plug my speaker into the outlet," she said.

"W-a-a-i-i-t-t, Hope," her father yelled. But she didn't hear him. It was too noisy and crowded.

Hope plugged her speaker into an outlet by one of the Potato stands as the rain came down.

"N-o-o-o-o, Hope," yelled her father.

But it was too late. A few seconds later the electricity in the entire market went out.

Jarvais and the class were on the highest floor of the Potato Museum when they saw the lightning.

"Oh my, this is some different kind of rain. It's been a long time since it poured down like this," said Mrs Georgia Louise Peach.

The students were scared as they looked through the window. It was thundering hard.

"Oh, a little rain never hurt nobody," said Cee Celery.

At that moment, lightning struck again in Market City and everything in Potato Glow went dark. The entire city lost power.

Mr Uri and Mr Granda searched their pockets for lighters.

Everyone was worried, especially Cee Celery, who was shaking and screaming hysterically at the top of his lungs. "Get me out of here, someone please!"

The entire city had no power. The elevators and the doors wouldn't work. They were stuck in darkness, all afraid, except for Jarvais.

As soon as the power went out, something clicked in his mind. Mr Granda held the lighter in front of Jarvais and looked at him without saying anything. Jarvais knew exactly what needed to be done. He acted quickly.

"Don't be afraid, class. I got this. I got this for real. Mrs Louise Peach, we need as many pennies as you have in that purse of yours."

Jarvais then went around the entire room on the top floor, calling every Potato he could see.

"Come with me," he said to the various Potatoes. "Trust me. Just come."

They all followed him. "The only way this is going to work is if we come together. There's a LED clock on the desk behind the paintings. We have wires and all that we need."

Some of the Fruits and Vegetables were confused.

"Man, I think that fall really got to him," said Brea, shaking her head. "Jarvais has lost it."

"Come together," Jarvais called.

He made every Potato hold hands and connect. With a penny in one hand, and a wire in the other, the Potatoes all held on tightly to one another as Jarvais counted to ten. 1, 2, 3, 4, 5, 6 … by the time he got to 7 a tiny flash of light flickered in the room. By 8, more light entered and by 9, the darkness began to disappear. At the count of 10, power and electricity was completely restored all over Market City.

Jarvais Po saved the day. Everyone cheered and clapped for him. Jarvais had forgotten many things about himself over time but at that moment he remembered the power he had within as a Potato. Potatoes are very different, like Mrs Carrot had said. They're so unusually different from any other Fruit or Vegetables that they have the ability to create power and electricity. In times of darkness, it is a Potato that can help bring light. It's strange but scientifically true. How could Jarvais have let anyone make him forget how excellent he was. Many of us do that.

"I can't believe this. Now I know why they call it Potato Glow. Wait until I tell my Dad," said Brea.

"Oh, big deal," sneered Cee Celery. "Jarvais is still just a little brown funny-shaped stubbly Potato!"

flickers

At that moment, Jarvais walked right up to Cee Celery.

"You know what, Cee Celery, we Potatoes may look different but we don't all have to look the same to be kind to each other. I'm not gonna take your opinion as my truth anymore. I'm actually proud of who I am. I should never have let you make me feel bad about myself. I know who I am. I'm amazing and powerful. Every single Fruit and Vegetable brings benefit to the whole world. We're all powerful. So just leave me and everybody else alone!" Jarvais proclaimed in an assertive voice that no one had ever heard from him.

Everyone was shocked. Someone finally had the courage to say what they all wanted to say to Cee Celery.

Alvin Avocado turned to Jarvais and said, "Thank you, my friend."

Then Brea and Aaliyah gave Jarvais a hug and said, "Thank you."

"Thanks!" said Kauli Cauliflower as he shook Jarvais' hand.

Even Ella Eggplant turned to Jarvais and thanked him. So many of Jarvais' classmates thanked him for his courage.

He had no idea that so many others in the Garden Bunch were going through the exact same thing. This was not just another day in the secret adventures of a Potato and his friends. It was an extraordinary day and Jarvais was happy he had lived to experience it.

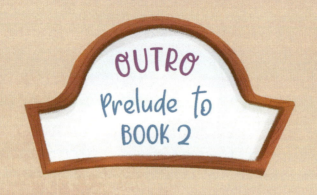

The Road to Broccoli City

Outside of the history museum, Rudy Rutabaga was losing his mind. He couldn't believe the power had gone out in Market City on a day when the media, as well as politicians from all over the world, were in town. He couldn't wait to fire his engineers. They cost him at least a few million dollars in that short amount of time and, even worse, his reputation was fractured. He knew the dishonest media would blame him. He screamed at Terry Turnip, "Oh, what a useless project manager you are. Tell these men to go back to Broccoli City with all those useless Broccolis and come up with a better source of generating power in my buildings! I can't afford mistakes. I'm too close to taking control. I can't wait until all these cities are mine!" he screamed. "Mine, mine, mine!"

Acknowledgments

This book is dedicated to all my teachers, Mrs Williams, Ms Teague, Mr Granda, Mr Uri, Mr Deluca, Dr Hudlin, Dr Ellison and many more.

To my parents, Grace and Dr George, Aunty Vi and all who left too soon, your love and lessons remain.

To my family, and the friends who became family, thank you.

To Diamon & Zindoga, thank you deeply for your creativity and time. You belong, and are a piece of this beautiful puzzle.

Gamili, Keisha, Sand, Edmund, Shona, Queen Taese and family, you lent me your ear and your time during this process.

Thank you, Ms J and Team EmpowHer for strengthening me.

Thank you so much, Fuuji. I couldn't have asked for a better collaborator.

To my readers, grief is painful. Life can be difficult but this is for all the laugher we didn't miss and to all the sunsets we lived to see.

May we always find the power to see another tomorrow.
It is there that joy resides.

About the Author

Abesi Manyando is a creative soul, artist and writer in love with poetry, laughter and wordplay. She is obsessed with humanity, earth, nature and gardens. Abesi is convinced that with unconditional love and support any of us can bloom to our highest selves.

Favorite quote: Until the lion has its own storyteller, the hunter will always be the hero of the story.

Made in the USA
Columbia, SC
11 March 2021

34255434R00038